Also By Jennifer Holik

The Tiger's Widow

Stories of the Lost

Engaging the Next Generation: A Guide for Genealogy Societies and Libraries

Branching Out: Genealogy for Adults

Branching Out: Genealogy for High School Students

Branching Out: Genealogy for 4th-8th Grades Students

Branching Out: Genealogy for 1st-3rd Grade Students

To Soar with the Tigers

Stories From The Battlefield:
A Beginning Guide to World War II Research

Written by Jennifer Holik

Generations Publishing

Copyright Information

Copyright © 2014 Jennifer Holik
Publisher: Generations, Woodridge, Illinois

All rights reserved. No part of this book may be reproduced or transmitted in any form or by any means, electronic or mechanical, including photocopying, recording, or by any information storage or retrieval system without written permission from the author, except for the inclusion of brief quotations in a review.

Editor: Heather Gates Reed

Cover Designer: Sarah Sucansky. Cover image of military funeral at Hamm Cemetery (now Luxembourg) courtesy of the American Battle Monuments Commission.

Holik, Jennifer, 1973 –
    Stories from the Battlefield: A Beginning Guide to World War II Research / Jennifer Holik. Includes bibliographical references and indexes.

ISBN: 1499754299
ISBN-13: 978-1499754292

Printed in the United States of America

R0443608516

Dedication

This book is dedicated to Mike Boehler, David Metherell, and Robert Rumsby, my colleagues and friends. Through their research, and dedication to the missing and living, they help ensure our World War II soldiers are not forgotten.

Acknowledgements

This book could not have been written without the support of several people. First to my boys, Andrew, Luke, and Tyler. Thank you for your support, love, and patience, while I continue to research and write my books.

Thank you Robert Rumsby, Mike Boehler, David Metherell, and Scott Lyons for introducing me to new aspects of World War II research every day. I am grateful for the friendship and conversation.

To Jennifer Alford and Shannon Combs Bennett, thank you for being beta readers for this book. Your comments and suggestions were extremely helpful.

A big thank you to Teri Embrey, Chief Librarian, and Paul Grasmehr, Reference Coordinator, of the Pritzker Military Museum and Library, for always being so helpful and supporting and patiently answering all my questions. You both make the research and writing much easier for me.

To my Pritzker Military Museum and Library YPA friends, Jason Camlic, Bob Haas, and Wendy Palmer. Thank you for your love, support, and encouragement through all my projects.

I am very grateful to Norm Richards, a historian for the 90th Division Association, for his dedication in helping me locate records at the National Personnel Records Center. Also for answering every question I ever asked about military records. I could not do the work I do without your assistance.

Thank you to my cover designer Sarah Sucansky for another amazing cover. Thank you to my outstanding editor Heather Gates Reed for her editing skills and guidance.

Table of Contents

1 Introduction	15
The Purpose of this book	16
2 Basics of Military Research	19
Military Research Checklist	20
Start with the Basics	20
Military Service Questionnaire	22
Locating a Service Number	24
Cemetery Information	25
Locate Home Sources	26
3 Requesting the Official Military Personnel File	29
The Official Military Personnel File	30
Requesting the OMPF	32
Women in the Red Cross and USO	33
Red Cross Records	33
United Service Organization	34
Next Steps	34
4 Organizational Records	47
Important Documents to Search	48
Morning Reports	49
After Action Reports	49
Air Force Accident Reports	50
Missing Air Crew Reports	51
General Orders & Field Orders	52
Staff Reports	52
Unit Histories	52
Correspondence	53
Photographs, Maps, and Aerial Photography	53
Publications	54
Next Steps	54
5 Military Death Records	61
Individual Deceased Personnel File and X-File Contents	63
Requesting IDPFs	65
Example IDPF Request Letter	65
Military Headstone Application	66
6 After The War	75
For More Information and Advanced Research	76

Selected Resources	79
World War II Toolbox	80
Books	80
Index	81
About the Author	83
Books By Author	84

1
Introduction

World War II was a conflict that ravaged much of the globe between 1939 and 1945. It affected a generation of people who witnessed and experienced extreme danger on the front lines and changed technology, the roles of men and women at home, and created a new way of living for many around the world. In the U.S., this generation of soldiers and home front supporters were dubbed "The Greatest Generation."

It is important to realize while the Greatest Generation suffered many losses and their lives were drastically changed, those changes trickled down to future generations. The men and women who lived through the hell of war changed and shaped the way we view war today. Their actions and work laid the foundation for those in subsequent generations to have more choices, especially women. Have you ever stopped to consider how the results of World War II affect today's generation?

Do we really need to understand the service and sacrifice of the greatest generation to live today? Yes we do, and to discover the answer we need to ask ourselves what can we learn by studying the past? Specifically, how can understanding the roles of our WWII-era ancestors help us navigate our lives today?

Families were changed during the war as men and women left to fight and never return. Children grew up fatherless or with a step-father. Women became young widows who had to navigate being a single parent and breadwinner. The sacrifice of these men and women allow us to live free in a country with meaningful civil liberties. The women who served laid the foundation for women to have additional choices outside of marriage. The actions of a father in World War II may have led to his sons and grandsons choosing to join the military to continue in their ancestor's footsteps. It is my hope you will begin a journey into the past to discover the lives of your WWII-era ancestors and really explore their stories.

The Purpose of this book

This guide is meant to be a starting point for World War II research, not an exhaustive examination of all the military branches and records available. In a few months I will release the first volume of a new book series providing an in-depth look all the branches of the military and the major records and resources you can find for each. The first book is called, Stories from the Battlefield Volume I: Navigating World War II Home Front, Civilian, Army, and Air Corps

Introduction 17

Records. Future volumes will round out the exploration of remaining branches during World War II.

I have been researching military personnel for many years. Repeatedly, I have been told by novice researchers, 'the records burned and there is nothing I can do to find the information.' This is not true.

Yes, there was a fire in 1973 at the National Personnel Records Center. Yes, 80% of the Army and Air Corps records burned. However, there are other record sources which allow you to trace a soldier's service from enlistment to discharge or death.

The problem is the genealogical books considered standard reading for anyone learning how to research in this field are out of date and were published between 2004 and 2010. There are currently no current books available which discuss all the record options available to researchers.

There is also the assumption WWII service records are still under lock and key at the National Personnel Records Center (NPRC) and available only to the veteran or next-of-kin. This too is no longer true. These records were made publicly available within the last few years if a soldier was discharged or died by 1952. If your soldier served in WWII and stayed in the military after and served post-1952, those records are still only available by the veteran or next-of-kin. Who is considered a next of kin if the veteran is deceased? The next of kin can be any of the following:

Surviving spouse that has not remarried
Father
Mother
Son
Daughter
Sister
Brother

As next of kin you must provide proof of death in the form of a death certificate, obituary, funeral cards or other documentation.

If your soldier's service records did burn, there are many other sources through which you can tell his or her story. It requires patience, deeper research, and creativity but it can be done. If you read James Privoznik's story in my book, Stories of the Lost, you will see no service records referenced in the notes. His records burned. Yet through photos, family stories, and other sources, I traced his entire service. Are there some gaps? Of course! But overall, the story is there.

Are you ready to begin?

Researching a military ancestor begins the same as researching any other ancestor. We start with the facts we "know" and the sources we have at home. Next we add in the basics of military research which will be discussed in the following chapter.

2

Basics of Military Research

20 *Basics of Military Research*

Figuring out where to start your military research should not be a daunting task. Instead it should be viewed as an adventurous journey through which you will likely travel to different countries, experience new things, and connect with your ancestors. To help you navigate this journey, use the checklist provided below as a map for your starting point to your destination, the telling of your soldier's story.

Military Research Checklist

The following is a list of records and resources for your research. This is not an exhaustive list of available items, but a beginning list to get you started. Each will be discussed in more detail through this book. Use the list as a step-by-step guide to move your research forward. You will learn which items on the checklist applied to your soldier, and which did not as you read this book.

- After Action Reports
- Air Force Accident Reports
- Cemetery Information
- Correspondence
- Discharge or Separation Papers
- Family Stories
- Genealogical Information
- General Orders
- Home Sources
- Individual Deceased Personnel File (IDPF)
- Military Service Questionnaire
- Missing Air Crew Reports (MACR)
- Morning Reports (MR)
- Official Military Personnel File (OMPF)
- Photographs and Maps
- Publications
- Staff Reports
- Unit Histories

Start with the Basics

Family stories are one of the first places we obtain information about our military ancestors and it is imperative we write these stories down. Even conflicting stories have grains of truth in them that need to be evaluated against other stories and sources.

An example from my family is that of Frankie Winkler. The family lore stated Frankie spoke German and was in reconnaissance.

He was a member of the 29th Infantry Division which came ashore on D-Day at Omaha Beach. Frankie received head wounds during the invasion and died a few weeks later of those wounds. When his remains were returned to the family, his father and uncle did not believe them to be Frankie's. Frankie's mother Jennie said she would bury this boy even if it wasn't her son and hope that another mother was burying her son.

That is an interesting story yet all the basic facts we need are not provided. The only two things we know for sure are Frank's name and his unit. Even the unit could be somewhat incorrect because soldiers often served in multiple units during the war. This story illustrates one point in time, the invasion of France on June 6, 1944.

What pieces of the puzzle are missing that would enable us to begin a search? First, we do not have a serial number for Frankie. Next we need places and dates of service; his death date and location; place of burial; and other service history. Most of this information may be contained in your genealogical information and home sources.

To help you begin your search for a soldier, complete the Military Questionnaire on the following pages with as much information as possible. It is alright if you do not know all the answers when you begin. Do you know the soldier's serial number? Do you have a copy of the veteran's Separation Paper or Discharge Paper? Do you have the Individual Deceased Personnel File (IDPF) if the soldier died while in service?

Military Service Questionnaire

It is important to complete as much of the form on the following page as possible. You can download this form off my website: http://jenniferholik.com under the World War II Toolbox General Resources.

The information may be found on the Separation/Discharge Paper issued to the soldier upon the end of his or her service. Information may also come from family sources and the Individual Deceased Personnel File (IDPF). It is important to document the source where you located each piece of information.

Military Service Questionnaire

Basic Information

Name of Soldier _____

Serial Number _____

Branch of the service _____

Unit(s) and dates of service _____

_____

Date of and Place of Birth _____

_____

Names of parents _____

Name of spouse (if applicable) _____

Service Information

Date and place of enlistment _____

Address at enlistment _____

_____

Date and place of separation _____
    Type of Separation: Honorable   Dishonorable

Address at discharge/separation _____

_____

Date and Place of Death _____

_____

    If soldier was killed in action, temporary burial location:

_____

Permanent burial date and place: _____

_____

Was soldier ever declared Missing in Action? Please provide details.

_____

Was soldier ever a Prisoner of War? Please provide details.

_____

Battles _____

_____

Service outside continental U.S. _____

_____

Ships on which the soldier served or was transported, with dates

_____

Decorations and Citations. Please provide the battles, reason(s), and dates for each decoration or citation received.

_____

_____

Wounds received _____

Prior Service _____

Training

Military Occupational Specialty (MOS) _____

Service Schools Attended _____

_____

24 *Basics of Military Research*

Post-World War II Information

Additional Service after WWII _____

_____

Did the soldier belong to any veterans or military organizations post-WWII? List those. _____

_____

Additional Remarks _____

_____

Discuss what you know about this soldier's service and what questions you have. Please list all the documents you have obtained and major resources searched. (American Battle Monuments Commission website, Unit Histories, Morning Reports, After Action Reports, S-Journals, Maps, IDPFs, X-Files)

_____
_____

Locating a Service Number

What happens when you do not have a Soldier's Discharge Papers, do not know his serial number, or unit? You can contact the National Personnel Records Center in St. Louis by letter and ask them to search the VA Index. (Form 180 will not work for this request.) The VA Index is an index of all service members. The cards will provide the following information on a soldier:

Name
Address upon discharge or death
Serial Number
Rank
Birth date
Enlistment, Discharge, and/or death date
Last unit in which he/she served

If Your Soldier Survived the War

After receiving a copy of the VA Index Card you can continue your search by attempting to obtain the Separation Paper or Discharge Paper which is contained in the Official Military Personnel

Files (OMPF.) There are two places you may find Separation and Discharge papers outside of your home.

First, contact the County Recorder or County Clerk in the county in which the soldier lived after the war. Returning veterans were encouraged to file their Separation and Discharge papers with the County offices for safekeeping. Second, send in Form 180 which you can obtain from the NPRC website (http://www.archives.gov/veterans/) and request a copy of the service file if it still exists. You also have the option to request an appointment at the NPRC and request the file(s) you wish to view and visit in-person.

If Your Soldier Died in the War

If your soldier was killed in action or died of wounds received during his service, a document called the Individual Deceased Personnel File (IDPF) was created. You can obtain a copy of this file by writing to the U.S. Army Human Resources Command. An example letter and the address for the U.S. Army Human Resources Command are in the chapter on Military Death Records.

Cemetery Information

In addition to requesting the IDPF, you should request information from the cemetery if your soldier was repatriated after the war and buried in the United States. The cemetery plot details will provide the interment date which will be 1947 or later if your soldier died overseas.

If your soldier is or might be buried overseas, search the American Battle Monuments Commission (ABMC) website (http://abmc.gov) for a burial record. Upon locating your soldier in an overseas cemetery, you can write to the cemetery and request a photo of the grave. ABMC will send you, free of charge, a lithograph size photo of the cemetery with a photo of your soldier's grave in the corner. This request also takes several weeks to process so mark your calendar.

Locate Home Sources

Now that you have completed the military questionnaire, it is time to explore the many possible resources with your home or the homes of your relatives in which you might locate additional clues to military service.

Badges
Bibles
Burial Flags in Cases
Cemetery Records
Church Records
Company Newsletters
Diaries & Journals
Draft Registration Cards
Employment Records
Family Genealogies
Family Medical Records
Fraternal Organization Records
Funeral Books
Funeral or Mass Cards
Headgear
Headstones and Markers
Home Movies
Identification Tags
Insignia
Insurance Records
Letters
Memorial Notices
Military Citations
Military Equipment
Military Medals & Ribbons
Military Medical Records
Military Separation Papers
Military Uniforms
Navy Cruise Books
Newspaper Articles
Obituaries
Pension Records
Photographs
Postcards
Probate Records
School Records
Scrapbook
State-Level War Participation Certificate
Uniform Buttons
Uniform Patches
Unit Association Websites (Reunion materials)
Unit Awards
Unit Histories
Unit Newsletters Created Overseas
Unit Photographs
V-Mail
VFW and Other Veteran Group Records
Wartime Telegrams
Weapons
Wedding Album
World War II Bonus Applications
World War II History Books

Basics of Military Research 27

```
AMOROSO, VITO VICTOR          XC22108705
Pvt.                           C
                               K
933 S. Hoyne Ave.,
Chicago, Ill.                  NN19714056

Sn   46-048-584  Died  4/9/63  V

Born 11-15-26                  A

Enl 1-9-46       Dis 4/11/47

VETERANS ADMINISTRATION
Form 7202a—(Rev. May 1944)
          MASTER INDEX CARD
```

Vito Victor Amoroso VA Index Card. National Personnel Records Center, St. Louis, Missouri.

3

Requesting the Official Military Personnel File

Armed with as much information as possible, the next step is to initiate a search for the Official Military Personnel file (OMPF) if you have not already done so. How you initiate a search depends slightly on which branch of the military your soldier belonged.

> **TIP!** Women served in all branches of the military during World War II. Their service records and organizational records are held in the same place you will find men's service records. Records for those who aided the war effort by working with the Red Cross or USO are addressed separately.

The Official Military Personnel File

The Official Military Personnel File (OMPF) was created for every individual who served in the armed forces. OMPF records are generally the same but each branch has some differences. The full service file contents vary soldier to soldier and also branch to branch. One soldier's file may contain more paperwork than another depending on the branch of the military, the type of training received, and the rank of an individual. These records were not duplicated and do not exist on microfilm or in any other repository outside of the NPRC.

Some researchers make claims that the entire service file is included in the IDPF of a deceased soldier. This is simply untrue. The IDPF may contain physical examination information along with brief statements of training and duty locations, enlistment date and place, and next of kin information but not an entire service record.

The same is true for a service record. If a soldier was killed in service, components of his IDPF may be included in the OMPF. These items range from telegrams, statements of death, witness information concerning a Missing in Action or Prisoner of War status, and other pieces of the IDPF but rarely the entire file.

All paperwork within a soldier's file contains his name and serial number. In general, the OMPF is a valuable resource to gather the following information.

Enlistment Records. This record details when and where a soldier volunteered or was drafted for duty.

Physical Examination Records. These pages contained information on vaccines given; physical exams; illnesses and operations (former and current); and vision and dental details for a soldier. If a soldier was killed in action, these records may have been included in their IDPF.

Pay records. Each man carried a Soldier's Individual Pay Record book with him or with the unit. In this was a record of the pay he received during enlistment. This information may be found in a service record.

Medical records. These are not the same as Physical Examination Records. These records contain details concerning physical or mental treatment administered to a soldier overseas or stateside.

Special Orders. Special Orders are records issued by higher commands indicating changes in duty or the award of a medal or citation.

Applications for Training. In one Army Officer's OMPF there exists an Application for Pilot Training in Office Grade Reserve and National Guard A.U.S. This particular officer was applying to flight school and if accepted, would have been removed from the Army Infantry to the Army Air Corps as a pilot in training.

Duty Station Changes. These documents take a variety of forms depending on the branch of the military. They can be a Naval slip indicating when a Sailor or Marine was stationed on a particular ship or a letter from the headquarters of a division to his subordinate officers indicating who was to be transferred in or out of a unit.

Discharge Paper. The discharge paper contained the soldier's name; rank; last unit in which he served (this does not mean the only unit); citations and awards received; and location of discharge. These records also contained the length of time served overseas including which theater.

What is not found within the OMPF? Information on the battles and engagements in which the soldier was a part is not in the file. This information can be found through other sources such as the Morning Report, Unit Histories, and Journals. These resources are discussed in the next chapter.

Requesting the OMPF

Army, Army Air Corps (current day Air Force), Navy (including Armed Guard,) Coast Guard, Marine Corps, and federalized National Guard records are all held at the NPRC in St. Louis. There are three ways to access these records.

Mail in Form 180

The least expensive way to begin a search is to fill out Form 180 located on the NPRC website (http://archives.gov) and see if the file survived. If records are discovered, NPRC will send you a letter indicating such and your fee for copies. Form 180 will ONLY search personnel records.

National Personnel Records Center
1 Archives Drive
St. Louis, Missouri 63138

Visit NPRC In-Person

There are other records to assist your research beyond service files at the NPRC. Payroll records and Morning Reports are two common record sets used by researchers.

Hire a Researcher

Another option is to hire an independent researcher who knows their way around the NPRC records. There are many more valuable records at the NPRC besides the service files. You can find a researcher list on the NPRC website.

I highly recommend a man on that list whom I have personally worked with. His name is Norm Richards. He is efficient, quick, and answers all questions. Mr. Richards is also one of the historians for the 90th Division and is very knowledgeable. You can contact him at: nrichards2@juno.com. Tell him I referred you.

Non-Federalized National Guard Records

Non-Federalized National Guard records are held at the state level in a State Archives, State Military Museum, or State VA administration office. Check with your state to find out if they hold any records.

Merchant Marines Records

The Merchant Marines were a civilian organization except during wartime, when they fell under the Department of the Navy. Service members who survived the war have records available with discharges from the U.S. Coast Guard. You can write to the following address providing the information requested to request a search. Include the Name, Date of Birth, copy of Death Certificate if deceased, Social Security number, Address, and Z or Service number.

Commanding Officer
USCG-National Maritime Center (NMC-421)
ATTN: Correspondence Section
100 Forbes Drive
Martinsburg, WV 25404

To request records for service members who were killed during the war, write to the following address providing the information requested. Include the Name, Date of Birth, Date of Death, Social Security number, Address, and Z or Service number.

Old Navy/Maritime Reference
Archives I -Textual Services Branch
National Archives and Records Administration
700 Pennsylvania Avenue NW
Washington DC 20408

Women in the Red Cross and USO

Women not only served in every branch of the military but also joined the Red Cross and USO to support the war effort. Unfortunately, there is not one central repository for either organization's records. Locations of records are described within each section. You should also search http://worldcat.org or http://beta.worldcat.org/archivegrid/ to find out which institution might hold relevant information.

Red Cross Records

Many women supported the war effort by working for the Red Cross. The Red Cross organization is the first place you should inquire about records and history. Next, search educational facilities, newspapers, newsletters, company records, home sources, and the National Archives. Additional sources you should look at include oral histories and books written about the Red Cross or by former Red Cross workers.

United Service Organization

The United Service Organization (USO) was founded by President Franklin D. Roosevelt in 1941to provide emotional support to the troops. It accomplished this through the creation of traveling shows that went to all theaters of war. USO Canteens were also established where off-duty officers and enlisted men could eat, be entertained, write letters home, or just relax.

USO Records may be scattered throughout various libraries and archives. The New York Public Library has a collection donated by the USO Camp Shows. This collection holds history of the USO, photographs, and show information. Other sources to check include oral histories, and military museums and bases. Some institutions, like the Air Force Museum in Dayton, Ohio, have exhibits on USO shows and performers.

Next Steps

There are many other records which were created during WWII that are available for researchers. The next chapter discusses some of the organizational records created during the war.

Armed Forces' Original
D. S. S. Form 221
January 30, 1942

BUDGET BUREAU No. 83-R030
Approval expires September 30, 1943

Local Board No. 112
Chicago City

NOV 10 1942

3336 W. 26th Street
Chicago, Illinois

REPORT OF PHYSICAL EXAMINATION AND INDUCTION

(LOCAL BOARD DATE STAMP WITH CODE)

First examination [X]   Second examination [ ]   Third examination [ ]   Fourth examination [ ]
(To be filled in by local board clerk. Check number of examination made by local board)

SECTION I.—GENERAL (To be filled in by the local board clerk from the Selective Service Questionnaire, D. S. S. Form 40. Write "none" opposite the questions where no information is given. Do not leave any question blank.)

	Do Not Enter Anything in This Column
	(To be filled in by Armed Forces)
1. Name (page 1) JOSEPH JOHN HOLIK / 942 9146	RESIDENCE
(First) (Middle) (Last) (Armed Forces Serial No.)	State
2. Address (page 1) 3114 S. RIDGEWAY AVE. CHICAGO COOK ILL	
(Street or rural route) (Town or city) (County) (State)	County
3. Social Security No. (Series I, line 5) .... 4. Registrant's order number (page 1) V-1856	
5. Physical or mental defects or diseases (Series II, line 1) None	Place Inducted
6. Treatment at an institution, sanitarium, or asylum (Series II, line 2) No	
(Yes or no)	
7. Education (Number years completed) (Series III): Elementary school 8 High school 2 Vocational school, college, or university 0	DATE INDUCTED
8. Occupation: (a) Title of present job (Series IV, line 2 (a), or Series V, line 1) Package handler	Day
(b) Duties (Series IV, line 2 (b)) Sort packages	Month
(c) Title of last job, if unemployed (Series IV, line 3)	Year
9. Years experience in this work (Series IV, line 2 (c), or Series V, line 2) 2½ Months	Source
10. Income (Series IV, line 2 (d)): Average Weekly earnings $ 22.00	
(Weekly, monthly, annual)	Nativity
11. Employment class (Series IV, line 2 (e)): Permanent employee [X]; Temporary employee [ ]; Apprentice [ ]; Independent worker [ ]; Unpaid family worker [ ]; Employer [ ]; Student (Series IV, line 4 (a)) [ ]	
12. Business of present employer (Series IV, line 2 (g)) Handling Express Packages	Year of birth
13. Marital status (Series VII, line 1): Single [ ]; Widower [ ]; Divorced [ ]; Married, not separated [X]; Married, separated [ ]	Race/citizenship
14. Number of dependents (Series VII, line 3 (a) fifth column except N. C.'s plus line 4 (a) fifth column) 4	
15. Birthplace (Series IX, line 1) Chicago Illinois U.S.A.	Education
(Town or city) (State) (Country)	
16. Birth date (Series IX, line 2) March 17th 1906	Occupation
(Month) (Day) (Year)	
17. Race (Series IX, line 3): White [X]; Negro [ ]; Other (specify)	Marital
18. Citizenship: United States citizen (Series IX, line 4) Yes ; Declarant alien (Series IX, line 7)	
(Yes or no) (Yes or no)	
19. Previous U. S. military service (Series XII): None [X] Army [ ]; National Guard [ ]; Navy [ ]; Marine Corps [ ]; Coast Guard [ ]	
20. Type of discharge (Series XII): Specify None	
21. Date of registrant's affidavit (top of page 8) 16th June 1941	
(Day) (Month) (Year)	

INSTRUCTIONS

1. An original and three copies of this form will be prepared for each registrant called up for physical examination. The original is designated as the Armed Forces' Original; the first carbon copy, the National Headquarters' Copy; the second carbon copy, the Surgeon General's (Army)—Bureau of Medicine and Surgery (Navy)—Commandant Marine Corps (M. C.) Copy; and the third carbon copy, the Local Board's Copy. Instructions are contained on each copy.
2. Forms of men rejected by the armed forces will be marked "Rejected by the Armed Forces" in large letters at the top of page 1.
3. If the registrant is not sent to the induction station of the armed forces, or is rejected by the induction station of the armed forces, this original will be filed, along with the Local Board's Copy (3d copy), in the registrant's Cover Sheet (Form 53).
4. For registrants accepted by the induction station of the armed forces: If inducted by the Army, this original accompanied by F. B. I. Military Fingerprint Card will be forwarded from induction station to The Adjutant General, Washington, D. C.; if inducted by the Navy or Coast Guard, this original will be forwarded through the Main Recruiting Station to the Bureau of Navigation, Washington, D. C.; if inducted by the Marine Corps, this original will be sent to the Commandant, Headquarters, U. S. Marine Corps, Washington, D. C.
5. Fingerprints are required only on this original and only for registrants who are inducted. If inducted by the Army, prepare F. B. I. Military Fingerprint Card.

ORIGINAL COPY   (PAGE 1)

Official Military Personnel File, Report of Physical Examination and Induction Joseph J. Holik, U.S. Naval Reserve Serial No. 9429146. National Personnel Records Center, St. Louis, Missouri.

SECTION II.—REPORT OF LOCAL BOARD EXAMINING PHYSICIAN AND LOCAL BOARD CLASSIFICATION.

22. If registrant's answer to Item 6 above is "yes," when and for what ailment(s) ____

23. Is registrant now or previously an enrollee in the Civilian Conservation Corps: No ☐; Yes ☐
24. Serological test (syphilis): Date 11/10/43 Result KAHN TEST NEGATIVE
    Second serological test (syphilis): Date ____ Result ____
25. Examining physician's remarks: ____

26. (a) Do you find that the above-named registrant has any of the defects set forth in Part I of the List of Defects (Form 220)?
    (If in doubt, answer "no," and give details.) ____ If answer is "yes," describe the defects, in order of significance
    (Answer yes or no)

    (b) Do you find that the above-named registrant has any of the defects set forth in Part II of the List of Defects (Form 220)?
    (If in doubt, answer "no," and give details.) ____ If answer is "yes," describe the defects, in order of significance
    (Answer yes or no)

    (c) I have examined the above-named registrant in accordance with Selective Service Regulations.
    (d) Signature of examining physician ____
    (e) Place CHICAGO   COOK   ILL.   (f) Date 11/10/43
        (Town or city)   (County)   (State)

27. (a) This Local Board has classified the above-named registrant in Class 1-A
    (b) Signature of Member of Local Board ____
    (c) Place CHICAGO   COOK   ILL.   (d) Date ____
        (Town or city)   (County)   (State)

SECTION III.—NEAREST RELATIVE, PERSON TO BE NOTIFIED IN CASE OF EMERGENCY, AND DESIGNATION OF BENEFICIARY (To be filled out at the induction station of the armed forces for only those registrants accepted for military service.)
A. Nearest relative and person to be notified in case of emergency:
28. Nearest relative Mae Privoznik
    (Other than wife or minor child. Name in full)
29. Relationship sister   30. Address 3124 S. Ridgeway Ave., Chicago, Ill.
    (Number and street or rural route; if none, so state) (City, town, or post office) (State or country)
31. Person to be notified in case of emergency Libbie Barbara Holik
    (Name in full)
32. Relationship wife   33. Address 3114 S. Ridgeway Ave., Chicago, Ill.
    (If friend, so state) (Number and street or rural route; if none, so state) (City, town, or post office) (State or country)
B. Designation of beneficiary:
34. The persons eligible to be my beneficiary are designated below:
    (1) Libbie Barbara Holik - see above
        (Full name of wife; if wife, or if she is deceased or divorced, so state) (Wife's full address)
    (2) Joseph Frank, born 3/3/31 - Robert Joseph, 7/15/33 - Richard
        Thomas, 12/19/35 - same as wife's
        (Full name and address of each minor child and each dependent child over 21 years of age. If there are no children, so state. If the address is the same as the wife's, so state. Do not repeat address)
35. In the event of my leaving no widow or child, or their decease before payment is made, I then designate as my beneficiary the dependent relative whose name, relationship, and address are shown below:
    (3) Mae Privoznik - sister - see above
        (If designation of beneficiary is declined, man must state in own handwriting: "I decline to designate any person as my beneficiary")
36. In the event of the death or disqualification of the last-named dependent relative before payment is made, I then designate as my beneficiary the dependent relative whose name, relationship, and address are shown below:
    (4) Anna Rendak - sister - 3138 S. Millard Ave., Chicago, Ill.
        (If beneficiary is named in lieu of naming of alternate is declined, man must state in own handwriting: "I decline to designate an alternate beneficiary")

37. Signature of registrant Joseph   John   Holik
    (First name)   (Middle name)   (Last name)
38. Witnessed at NRS, Chicago, Illinois on Dec. 13, 1943, 19__
    (Signature of witness attesting)   H. B. Boaz, Ens., USN
    (Name of witness typed)   (Grade and organization)

ORIGINAL COPY   (PAGE 2)

Official Military Personnel File, Report of Physical Examination and Induction Joseph J. Holik, U.S. Naval Reserve Serial No. 9429146. National Personnel Records Center, St. Louis, Missouri.

SECTION IV.—PHYSICAL EXAMINATION RESULTS: (All Items Must Be Filled In. Indicate Normal or None Where Applicable. To Be Filled Out by the Medical Board at the Induction Station of the Armed Forces.)

		Do Not Write in This Column
39. Eye abnormalities ... n	60. Vision, without correction:	
	(a) Right eye 20/50	
40. Ear, nose, throat abnormalities healed perf. lt. ear drum	(b) Left eye 20/50	
	61. Vision, with correction:	
41. Mouth and gum abnormalities ... n	(a) Right eye 20/40	
	(b) Left eye 20/40	
42. Teeth: (a) Indicate restorable carious teeth by circling; nonrestorable carious teeth by /; missing natural teeth by X.	62. Color perception* n	
	63. Hearing:	
	(a) Right ear 15/15	
	(b) Left ear 15/15	
(b) Remarks, including other defects ... n	64. Height 70 inches.	
	65. Weight 179 pounds.	
(c) Prosthetic dental appliances partial denture replaces R-4-5-6-7-12-13-14-15, L-4-5-6-7-13-14-15	66. (a) Girth, at nipples; inspiration 43 inches.	
	(b) Girth, at nipples; expiration 40 inches.	
(d) Remediable dental defects ... n	(c) Girth, at umbilicus 37 inches.	
43. Skin ... n	67. Posture:	
44. Varicose veins ... n	Good ☐ Fair ☒ Poor ☐	
45. Hernia ... n	68. Frame:	
	Heavy ☒ Med. ☐ Light ☐	
46. Hemorrhoids ... n	69. Color of hair bro	
47. Genito-urinary (non-venereal) ... n	70. Color of eyes blu	
	71. Complexion rud	
48. Venereal diseases ... n	72. Pulse, sitting 76	
	73. Pulse, after exercise*	
49. Feet pes planus 2 deg. bil. N.S.	74. Pulse, 2 minutes after exercise*	
50. Musculoskeletal defects ... n	75. Blood pressure:	
	(a) Systolic 148	
51. Abdominal viscera ... n	(b) Diastolic 88	
	76. Urinalysis:	
52. Cardiovascular system ... n	(a) Specific gravity 1.012	
	(b) Albumin n	
53. Lungs ... n	(c) Sugar n	
	(d) Microscopic*	
54. Chest X-ray ... n	77. Other data:	
55. Mental ... n		
56. Nervous system ... n		
57. Endocrine system ... n		
58. Other defects and/or diseases or other remarks		
59. Summary of defects in order of significance		

*When indicated.

ORIGINAL COPY (PAGE 3)

Official Military Personnel File, Report of Physical Examination and Induction Joseph J. Holik, U.S. Naval Reserve Serial No. 9429146. National Personnel Records Center, St. Louis, Missouri.

SECTION IV.—PHYSICAL EXAMINATION RESULTS—Continued.

78. I CERTIFY that the above-named registrant was carefully examined, that the results of the examination have been correctly recorded on this form and that to the best of my knowledge and belief—

(a) __Joseph John Holik__ is physically and mentally qualified for general military service.
(Enter name of registrant if this subsection is applicable)

(b) _____ is physically and mentally qualified for general military service
(Enter name of registrant if this subsection is applicable)
after the satisfactory correction of the following remediable defects: _____

This registrant would have been accepted for general military service had the remediable defects herein specified been remedied at the time of this examination.

(c) _____ is physically qualified for limited military service only by
(Enter name of registrant if this subsection is applicable)
reason of _____

(d) _____ is physically qualified for limited military service after the
(Enter name of registrant if this subsection is applicable)
satisfactory correction of the following remediable defects: _____

This registrant would have been acceptable for limited military service had the remediable defects herein specified been remedied at the time of this examination.

(e) _____ is physically and/or mentally disqualified for military service by reason of
(Enter name of registrant if this subsection is applicable)

(f) _____ is disqualified for military service because of _____
(Enter name of registrant if this subsection is applicable)

(g) Signature _W. W. Smith_   (h) Title _Lt. MC-V(S) USNR_
                Medical Examiner.
(i) Name typed or stamped _W. W. Smith_

79. (a) _Joseph John Holik_ was this date inducted for (general; ~~limited~~) [strike out inapplicable
(Enter name of registrant if this subsection is applicable)
word] military service into the (fill in appropriate Service, such as Army, Navy, Marine Corps, or Coast Guard) _Navy_
_____ of the United States and sent to _NTS_

(b) _____ was this date rejected for service in the (fill in appropriate
(Enter name of registrant if this subsection is applicable)
service, such as Army, Navy, Marine Corps, or Coast Guard) _____ of the United States.
(c) Place _Chicago, Ill._   (d) Signature _H. B. Roaz_
(e) Date _Dec. 13, 1943_   (f) Name typed or stamped _H. B. Roaz, Ens. USN_
                                                                    (Grade and organization)

SECTION V.—LOCAL-BOARD CHANGE IN CLASSIFICATION AFTER EXAMINATION BY THE INDUCTION STATION OF THE ARMED FORCES.

80. (a) Based on the entries in (a), (c), (d), (e), or (f) of Item 78, above, the Local Board has changed the above-named registrant's classification to Class _____
(b) Based on the entries in (b) of Item 78, above, the Local Board has retained the above-named registrant in Class _____
(c) Place _____   (d) Date _____
(e) Signature of member of local board _____

FINGERPRINTS—RIGHT HAND

1. THUMB	2. INDEX	3. MIDDLE	4. RING	5. LITTLE

ORIGINAL COPY

Official Military Personnel File, Report of Physical Examination and Induction Joseph J. Holik, U.S. Naval Reserve Serial No. 9429146. National Personnel Records Center, St. Louis, Missouri.

APPLICATION FOR APPOINTMENT AND STATEMENT OF PREFERENCES FOR RESERVE OFFICERS
(SEE INSTRUCTIONS ON BACK)

From: White, Paul (none) Date January 10-, 1940
(Last name) (First name) (Middle name)

To: The Adjutant General, Washington, D. C.
(Through Corps Area or Department Commander)

I hereby make application for appointment as Second Lieutenant, Infantry
(Grade) (Section)
in the Officers' Reserve Corps.

In connection with the application I submit the following information, which I certify to be correct to the best of my knowledge:

1. Permanent address 1317 No. Wallace St. Indianapolis, Indiana

2. Date of birth May 7-1918 White or colored white
(Month) (Day) (Year)

3. Place of birth Indianapolis, Ind.

4. State whether or not you are a citizen of the United States and whether by birth or naturalization. (If the latter, append evidence of naturalization, or if evidence not available, state on what date and in what court naturalized.)
Citizen by birth

5. Married or single single

6. Number of minor children none

7. Name of nearest relative, giving relationship and address, including street and number:
John Ervin White Father
1317 No. Wallace St., Indianapolis, Ind.

8. Father's name White, John Ervin
(Last name) (First name) (Middle name)
Father's address 1317 No. Wallace St.
(Number and street, or rural route)
Indianapolis, Ind.
(City, town, or post office) (State or country)
Father's birthplace Indiana

If of foreign birth, state whether or not naturalized. (If naturalized, state on what date and in what court.)

Mother's name White, Joan --
(Present last name) (First name) (Middle name)
Mother's address same as father's
(Number and street, or rural route)

(City, town, or post office) (State or country)
Mother's birthplace Indiana

9. Marksmanship, giving year of qualification:
Rifle SS 1939
Pistol MM 1939

10. Languages:

	French	Spanish	German	Other	Other
Speaks fluently					
Speaks fairly	None				
Translates					
Reads					

11. Special knowledge, professional or other Forestry

12. Present occupation, years of experience in same and name and address of employer, if any Student about 9 yrs.

13. Experience in other lines and years of same Farming and truck driver during vacation

14. Schools attended, other than graded schools, including service schools:

Name of school	Number of years attended	Graduated? Yes or No	Year	Degrees
Arsenal HS Indianapolis, Ind.	4	yes	1935	
Butler Univ.	2	no		
O.S.A.C.	3	no	Will grad. June 1940	BS in For.

Subjects specialized in Wood Products

15. Campaigns and battles participated in (give dates) None

16. Decorations, citations, and commendations (attach copies) None

17. Wounds, giving date and place of occurrence None

18. State membership in professional societies None

19. Are you at present a member of the Regular Army, Enlisted Reserve Corps, or federally recognized in the National Guard? If so, state which, giving grade and organization or arm or service and date of expiration of enlistment:
No

W. D., A. G. O. Form No. 170
January 1, 1935

Official Military Personnel File, Application for Appointment and Statement of Preferences for Reserve Officers, Paul White, U.S. Army Serial Number O-391998. National Personnel Records Center, St. Louis, Missouri.

REPORT OF PHYSICAL EXAMINATION
(See AR 40-100 and AR 40-105)

INSTRUCTIONS.—Unless otherwise prescribed, this form will be used for all physical examinations of officers, nurses, or warrant officers; applicants for appointment as such in the Regular Army (R. A.), National Guard (N. G.), or Organized Reserve (O. R.); and enrollment in the Reserve Officers' Training Corps (R. O. T. C.). Indicate nature of examination and component of Army by underlining appropriate terms below. Nature of examination: Appointment, Promotion, Retirement, Annual, Active Duty, Special. Component of Army: R. A., N. G., O. R., R. O. T. C. Use typewriter if practicable. Attach additional sheets if required.

R.O.T.C.

1. White / Paul / / OSAC
   (Last name) (First name) (Middle initial) (Serial No.)
2. Cadet / / Age 20 / Years of service --
   (Grade) (Organization and arm or service) (Nearest birthday) (Whole number only)
3. Typhoid-paratyphoid vaccination: No. series completed 1   Last series April 22/39 19__
4. Date of last smallpox vaccination April 6/39   Type of reaction Immune
5. Other vaccinations or immunity tests None
6. Medical history Tonsillectomy 1922. No serious illness since last active duty

7. Eyes Normal
   Distant vision: Right 20/20 correctible to _____ by[1]
   (Snellen type) Left 20/20 correctible to _____ by[1]
   Near vision: Right J-1 correctible to _____ by[1]
   (Jaeger type) Left J-1 correctible to _____ by[1]
8. Color perception (red, green, and violet)[2] Normal
9. Ears Normal
   Hearing, low conversational voice: Right 20/20 left 20/20 Audiometer: Right ___ left ___
10. Nose and throat Normal
11. Teeth[3]: Right (Examinee's) Left
    U. 8 7 6 5 4 3 2 1 1 2 3 4 5 6 7 8   Indicate: Restorable carious teeth by O; nonrestorable carious teeth by /; missing natural teeth by X.
    L. 8 7 6 5 4 3 2 1 1 2 3 4 5 6 7 8
12. Remarks, including other defects None
    Classification IV
13. Prosthetic dental appliances None
14. Cardio-vascular system Normal
15. Blood pressure: S. 136, D. ____ Pulse rate: Sitting 78 Immediately after exercise 114
    Two minutes after exercise 84 Character Regular
16. Heart Normal
17. Respiratory system Normal
18. Posture Good   Figure Medium   Frame Medium
    (Excellent, good, fair, bad) (Slender, medium, stocky, obese) (Light, medium, heavy)
19. Height 71 inches. Weight 133 pounds. Chest: Inspiration 35 inches;
    expiration 32½ inches; rest 34 inches. Abdomen 27½ inches.
20. Bones, joints, and muscles Normal
21. Feet Pes Planus 1st deg.bilat   Skin Clear
22. Abdominal viscera Normal
23. Hernia None
24. Hemorrhoids None   Varicose veins None
25. Genito-urinary system Normal

[1] If annual physical examination, record only distant and near vision, and state whether defect is properly corrected.
[2] Not required for annual physical examination.
[3] If rejected for appointment in Regular Army because of malocclusion, send plaster models to The Surgeon General.

W. D., A. G. O. Form No. 63
May 15, 1929

Official Military Personnel File, Application for Appointment and Statement of Preferences for Reserve Officers, Paul White, U.S. Army Serial Number O-391998. National Personnel Records Center, St. Louis, Missouri.

REPORT OF PHYSICAL EXAMINATION
(See AR 40-100 and AR 40-105)

INSTRUCTIONS.—Unless otherwise prescribed, this form will be used for all physical examinations of officers, nurses, or warrant officers; applicants for appointment as such in the Regular Army (R. A.), National Guard (N. G.), or Organized Reserves (O. R.); and enrollment in the Reserve Officers' Training Corps (R. O. T. C.). Indicate nature of examination and component of Army by underlining appropriate terms below. Nature of examination: Appointment, Promotion, Retirement, Annual, Active Duty, Special. Component of Army: R. A., N. G., O. R., R. O. T. C. Use typewriter if practicable. Attach additional sheets if required.

1. _White_ , _Paul_ _J._ _____
   (Last name) (First name) (Middle initial) (Serial No.)
2. _____ _____ Age _21_ Years of service _____
   (Grade) (Organization and arm or service) (Nearest birthday) (Whole number only)
3. Typhoid-paratyphoid vaccination: No. series completed _1_ Last series _Apr._, 19_39_
4. Date of last smallpox vaccination _Apr. 1939_ Type of reaction _Immune_
5. Other vaccinations or immunity tests _none_
6. Medical history
   no serious illness.
   Tonsillectomy 1922.

7. Eyes _normal_
   Distant vision: Right _20/20_ correctible to _____ by¹
   (Snellen type) Left _20/20_ correctible to _____ by¹
   Near vision: Right _J.1_ correctible to _____ by¹
   (Jaeger type) Left _J.1_ correctible to _____ by¹
8. Color perception (red, green, and violet)² _normal_
9. Ears _normal_
   Hearing, low conversational voice: Right _20/20_ left _20/20_ Audiometer: Right _not taken_ left _taken_
10. Nose and throat _normal_
11. Teeth³: Right (Examinee's) Left
    U. 8 7 ⊗ 5 4 3 2 1 1 2 3 4 5 ⊗ 7 8
    L. 8 7 ⊗ 5 4 3 2 1 1 2 3 4 5 ⊗ 7 8
    Indicate: Restorable carious teeth by ○; nonrestorable carious teeth by /; missing natural teeth by ×.
12. Remarks, including other defects _none_
    Classification _IV_
13. Prosthetic dental appliances _none_
14. Cardio-vascular system _normal_
15. Blood pressure: S. _118_, D. _78_ Pulse rate: Sitting _76_ Immediately after exercise _110_
    Two minutes after exercise _78_ Character _Regular_
16. Heart _normal_
17. Respiratory system _normal_
18. Posture _Good_ Figure _Medium_ Frame _Medium_
    (Excellent, good, fair, bad) (Slender, medium, stocky, obese) (Light, medium, heavy)
19. Height _71_ inches; Weight _134_ pounds. Chest: Inspiration _35_ inches;
    expiration _32_ inches; rest _33½_ inches. Abdomen _28_ inches.
20. Bones, joints, and muscles _normal_
21. Feet _normal_ Skin _normal_
22. Abdominal viscera _normal_
23. Hernia _none_
24. Hemorrhoids _none_ Varicose veins _none_
25. Genito-urinary system _normal_

¹ If annual physical examination, record only distant and near vision, and state whether defect is properly corrected.
² Not required for annual physical examination.
³ If rejected for appointment in Regular Army because of malocclusion, send plaster models to The Surgeon General.

W. D., A. G. O. Form No. 63
May 15, 1929

Official Military Personnel File, Application for Appointment and Statement of Preferences for Reserve Officers, Paul White, U.S. Army Serial Number O-391998. National Personnel Records Center, St. Louis, Missouri.

26. Endocrine system: *normal*
27. Nervous system: *normal*
28. Laboratory procedures: Wassermann test *not indicated* Kahn test *not taken*
    Urinalysis: Sp. gr. *1.020* Albumin *none* Sugar *none*
    Microscopical (if indicated) *not indicated*
    Other laboratory procedures *none*
29. Remarks on defects not sufficiently described above *Health is very good. Firm muscle tone. An active individual who has a lower caloric intake than that required for the energy expended. Gains weight when not in school. X ray of chest reveals no pathology of heart or lungs. BP on Jan 31, 1940 = 118/78 & 114/78 p.m.*
30. Corrective measures, or other action recommended *" Feb 1, " = 114/80 & 116/74 "*
    Recommend: *" 2 " = 112/70 & 118/76 "*
    More rest. Higher caloric diet. Improve general hygiene.
31. Is the individual permanently incapacitated for active service? *no*
    If yes, specify defect
32. If applicant for appointment: Does he meet physical requirements? *no* Do you recommend acceptance with minor physical defects? *yes* If rejection is recommended, specify cause

Student Health Service O.S.C. *N. J. Stone, M.D.*, Corps.
(Place) *Corvallis, Oregon* (Name and grade)
(Date) *Feb. 2*, 19*40*. _____, Corps.
                          (Name and grade)
                          _____, Corps,
                          (Name and grade)

1st Ind.¹

Headquarters, _____, 19____
To the Commanding General, _____
Remarks and recommendations _____

_____
(Name)
_____ _____
(Grade)   (Organization and arm or service)
                                          Commanding.

2d Ind.¹

_____, 19____, To The Adjutant General.

3d Ind.¹

War Department, S. G. O., _____, 19____ To The Adjutant General.

Noted. See _____ Ind. Recommend

¹State action taken on recommendations of the board. If incapacitated for active service, state whether action by retiring board is recommended.

Official Military Personnel File, *Application for Appointment and Statement of Preferences for Reserve Officers*, Paul White, U.S. Army Serial Number O-391998. National Personnel Records Center, St. Louis, Missouri.

Left form (ORIGINAL)

Name: HOLIK, Joseph John

Service No.: 942 91 46 Rate: S1c., V-6, (SV)

Date Reported Aboard: 18 April 1944

Present Ship or Station: U.S.N., AGC, BROOKLYN, N.Y.

Ship or Station Received From: USN, AGS, GULFPORT, MISS.

6-20-44: Detached duty completed as armed guard on board U.S. Armed Merchant Vessel S.S. JOSHUA HENDY.

6-23-44: Trans. (Rcds & Accts) this date to USN, AGC, New Orleans, La.

AUTH: AGC/NOLA/L16-4/P20-2(Serial 8037) of 6-23-44.

Date Transferred: 6-23-44
To: USN, AGC, New Orleans, La.

[Signature] WM. M. COAKLEY, Comdr., USNR.

Date Received Aboard: 3 July 1944
ARMED GUARD CENTER, NOLA.
AGC, BROOKLYN, N.Y.

[Signature] L.V. TIMMINS, Lt. Comdr., USNR

ORIGINAL
FOR SERVICE RECORD

Right form (DUPLICATE)

020762

Name: HOLIK, Joseph John

Service No.: 942 91 46 Rate: S1c V-6 SV

Date Reported Aboard: 3, July 1944

Present Ship or Station: AGC, New Orleans, La.

Ship or Station Received From: AGC, Brooklyn, N.Y.

9, Sept. 1944 to DET:D. aboard the SS SEA QUAIL.

15, Jan. 1945 DET:D comp. aboard the SS SEA QUAIL AT AGC, Bklyn., NY.

22, Jan. 1945 TRAN: to AGC, Bklyn., N.Y.

AUTH: NM 22/AR/L16-4/P20-2/ser., 237, 19, Jan. 1945

Date Transferred: 22, Jan. 1945 (R&A)
To: AGC, Brooklyn, N.Y.

[Signature] Comdr. USNR

Date Received Aboard: 1/15/45
USN AGC BROOKLYN, N.Y.
AGC NEW ORLEANS, LA.

[Signature] Comdr. USNR

DUPLICATE
FOR BuPers ENLISTED MAN'S JACKET

Official Military Personnel File, Duty Station Changes, Joseph J. Holik, U.S. Naval Reserve Serial No. 9429146. National Personnel Records Center, St. Louis, Missouri.

44 The OMPF

Official Military Personnel File, Notice of Separation Joseph J. Holik, U.S. Naval Reserve Serial No. 9429146. National Personnel Records Center, St. Louis, Missouri.

Official Military Personnel File, Notice of Separation, Martin DeLeonardis, Army Serial No. 16144977. National Personnel Records Center, St. Louis, Missouri.

4

Organizational Records

48 *Organizational Records*

To paint a picture of a soldier's military service after analyzing the materials within the OMPF the next step is to look for organizational records. Some of these no longer exist within the National Archives records systems but may exist in personal collections, area museums, libraries and archives.

> **TIP!** Many Divisions are digitizing records related to service and placing these online on Division websites. A list of Division websites can be found on my World War II Toolbox on my website: http://jenniferholik.com

Important Documents to Search

After Action Reports
Air Force Accident Reports
Armed Guard Deck Logs
Biographies
Correspondence
Crew Lists (Naval & Coast Guard)
Duty Rosters
Field Manuals
Field Orders
General Orders
IDPFs
Maps
Marine Corps Muster Rolls
Marine Corps Ship Lists
Missing Air Crew Reports
Monthly Personnel Records
Morning Reports
Navy Cruise Books
Naval Deck Logs
Photographs
S-Journals
Ship Histories
Special Orders
Staff Reports
Submarine Log Books
Technical Manuals
Training Manuals
Unit Histories – Division Level
Unit Histories – Regimental Level
X-Files

Morning Reports

A Morning Report is a document created at the Company level each morning detailing the events of the prior day which ran from midnight to midnight. The Morning Report provides details on Company strength in numbers, location on that day, brief details about the weather and enemy engagement, and lists of those who entered and exited a unit with justification. Reasons included being transferred in, transferred out, Missing in Action, Wounded in Action, Killed in Action, Prisoner of War, and promotions.

You must know a soldier's unit down to the Company to initiate a search. Remember that the unit listed on a soldier's Separation Paper or in his IDPF is the final unit in which he or she served. It likely is not the only unit. This unit provides a starting point in time through which you can search Morning Reports.

Usually, but not always, the Company Clerk can indicate to which unit or from which unit a soldier was being transferred. In those cases, you can track a soldier's service from one point in time in either direction to enlistment or discharge. This is a valuable resource especially when the OMPF burned.

These records are held at the NPRC but you must go there in-person to search them or hire a researcher. Form 180 will not provide a search of Morning Reports.

After Action Reports

After Action Reports (A/A or AAR) are the next record you should seek. The AAR was created at the beginning of the month detailing a Division's location, movements, enemy interaction, and statistics on casualties, ordnance, and enemy engagement. These reports usually do not include the names of soldiers unless they are officers, but will provide historical context to help you better understand what your soldier may have been experiencing. This context may also lead you to additional histories and resources. The After Action Reports are held at the National Archives Branch in College Park, MD. You can view 90th Division After Action Reports here: http://www.90thdivisionassoc.org/History/AAR/index.html

Air Force Accident Reports

The Army Air Corps recorded every plane crash possible through a document called the Air Force Accident Report (AAR.) These records exist for both stateside accidents and overseas accidents. In cases where pilots or an entire crew crashed and were not immediately recovered, a Missing Air Crew Report (MACR) was completed. The AAR contained many documents and contents varied slightly depending on the place and date of a crash.

Within an AAR, we find a Report of Accident document which contains the names of all the crew on board with rank and serial number; type of plane flown; mission or training information; type and number of aircraft; location of the crash and airbase information.

The AAR also contained a description of the accident and witness reports if possible. Sometimes a crash occurred in a remote area where there were no witnesses. Many of the witness reports can be quite lengthy.

Not only are there witness reports but the War Department conducted a full investigation into the crashes. These reports contain information about the pieces of the plane discovered after the crash; type and location of any secret government equipment on the planes; scenarios of what caused the crash based on evidence; and a final determination as to fault of personnel or equipment.

Included with the reports are usually photographs of the crash scene. These photographs can be quite graphic and have been microfilmed. Copies included in an AAR are not of the highest quality but they do provide a lot of information about the crash.

In addition to photographs, maps often accompany the testimony or photographs to illustrate where a plane went down. Diagrams exist in some cases for the spread of wreckage.

There will usually be a summary of the entire accident that describes the crash; details on the crew; date and place of the crash; and a summary of events and outcomes.

> **Tip:** The AAR is usually indexed primarily by the pilot's name. Searching for a co-pilot or crew member may not be as easy. In those cases, you want to write to the National Archives or Aviation Archaeology (paid record site) to ask for a search of your crewmember, date of the accident or date range, location of accident, and any other information such as serial number and rank that you have on that individual.

Missing Air Crew Reports

A Missing Air Crew Report (MACR) was created when planes disappeared in training, combat, and as troop transports. Even if your soldier was not a pilot or crew member, if he or she disappeared or was shot down while traveling in an airplane, there should be a record. In my research, I have seen MACRs that list the flight crew plus doctors, nurses, and patients from all branches of the service. These records are worth investigating if your person was involved in a plane crash. What is included in a MACR?

MACRs, as other military records, contain standard documents but the contents vary based on the crash, location, and those involved. Crashes that occurred in German occupied areas might include some German documentation which will need to be translated if you do not speak German or it was not already translated within the full report.

MACRs provide the name, rank, serial numbers of all crew members and other aboard the aircraft. This includes any civilians if they were onboard. The location and details concerning the crash are also documented. Maps of the crash site, witness accounts of those who survived, were captured, or who rescued the downed individuals may also be included. Details on burial locations of deceased personnel are included. It includes any standard information that is found with an Air Force Accident Report which includes the plane information, secret equipment and guns carried, weather and circumstances of the crash. These records are held by the National Archives.

52 *Organizational Records*

> **Tip:** Fold3.com (a paid site) does have some MACRs available. The MACR is one place to begin looking for information on your lost serviceman or woman. From here you should request the service file and the IDPF if the soldier died as a result of the crash.

General Orders & Field Orders

General Orders (GO) record policies, procedures, promotions, and awards given to an individual or a unit. They detail key communications to a specific unit. General Orders can be used to trace promotions and awards to individuals if you have the unit to which that soldier belonged. These documents can be helpful when reconstructing a soldier's military career.

Field Orders (FO) was combat orders. These orders directed the action a unit was to take against the enemy and included who, what, when, and where for that order. These records are held within unit files at the National Archives. You can view examples on the 90th Division site: http://www.90thdivisionassoc.org/History/GO/index.html.

Staff Reports

Staff reports or journals, were created by four unit sections, Personnel (S-1), Intelligence (S-2), Operations, (S-3), and Supply (S-4). These records detailed the specific operations carried out by a unit and contained logs of incoming and outgoing correspondence and messages. If the records still exist, and many do not, they are held within the unit records at the National Archives.

Unit Histories

Unit histories are either written by the men who served in the unit or the branch of the service in which that unit existed. The official unit histories are held within each military branch's history departments at the National Archives in College Park, MD. Many have been digitized and are available online.

Histories written by the men who served may contain some embellishment of service details or provide some inaccurate dates when compared to official Morning Reports. Often, the sources of information contained within the history may not be cited leaving the reader to wonder where the information came from. Overall these histories are fairly accurate and provide another starting point for additional research. More important, they provide context for a soldier's story. These histories may be available online as digital downloads. See the 90th Division Website listed in the resources as an example of histories written by the men within that Division. You can view the 90th Division unit histories here as an example of what is included.

http://www.90thdivisionassoc.org/History/UnitHistories/index.html

Correspondence

Explore the correspondence kept by units. Correspondence could include messages to other commanders or personal correspondence of a soldier to his family. Soldiers could not describe specific battles or duty stations as these would be cut out by the military censor, but you still get an idea of their hopes, fears, and past enemy engagements. Correspondence may be held within unit records, military museum archives, local archives, university special collections, and private collections.

Photographs, Maps, and Aerial Photography

Photographs and maps are a huge resource for researchers because they illustrate what was happening during the war. Maps were created prior to and during the war to outline large and small scale maneuvers and to provide a guide to soldiers and reconnaissance troops to navigate their way through various countries. Maps illustrate engagements in which your soldier participated and add to the story. Photographs and maps provide context through which we can find further information or tell a soldier's story.

There are some specific photos to look for which include:

Soldier Photos. These might be a single soldier or a unit photo. Pay particular attention to the uniform, location of the photo, airplanes, vehicles, and other evidence that might identify the people in addition to what they were doing.

Tourist Photos. Sailors and soldiers were granted leave or liberty now and then. Some carried cameras and played tourist for a few hours. You might discover photographs of Pompeii in Italy, local people or soldiers, churches, the ocean, and the landscape. This type of photo offers a glimpse of what life was like when your soldier was not fighting. Pay attention to the dates and locations of the photographs to add to a timeline of service especially if the service file burned.

Bombing and Mission Photos. Look for photos that depict missions or bombing raids. These provide an idea of what your pilot or navigator in a bomber saw and was supposed to do in the war.

Publications

One source of materials that will not talk about your soldier but provide context for a story are military publications in the form of Field Manuals, Technical Manuals, and Training Manuals. These manuals, many of which have been digitized, provided a soldier with the necessary training he or she needed to function in the military, use a weapon or other equipment, and do the job for which they were being trained.

Additional publications are *YANK Magazine* and the *Stars and Stripes* newspaper. In these publications, you may not find your soldier listed, but you can still gain some context to his story. YANK Magazine did publish poems, stories, and photos submitted by soldiers, so you may find something on your soldier. There are some digitized copies of these publications available online and some major libraries, university special collections, and military museums also hold physical copies.

Next Steps

If your soldier died in service, a file called the Individual Deceased Personnel File (IDPF) or an X-File was created. The IDPF was created for those who were identified. The X-File is essentially an IDPF for those who were unidentified. Details about these files are found in the next chapter.

Company Morning Report for Co. "G", 115th Infantry Regiment, 29th Infantry Division dated 4 July 1944. National Personnel Records Center, St. Louis, Missouri.

56 Organizational Records

```
                            CONFIDENTIAL

                         WAR DEPARTMENT
                    HEADQUARTERS ARMY AIR FORCES
                            WASHINGTON
                                              Classification changed
                                              to  RESTRICTED
                     MISSING AIR CREW REPORT        Lt. Col., AC
                                              by P. W. ash H, Capt., AC
                                              date    MAR

   1. ORGANIZATION: Location by Name  Tanauan   ; Command or Air Force  5th AF
      Group 433rd T. C.  ; Squadron  69th T. C. ; Detachment
   2. SPECIFY: Place of Departure  Elmore (Mindoro)  ; Course Elmore to Tanauan
      Target or Intended Destination Tanauan (Leyte) ; Type of Mission  Air Evac.
   3. WEATHER CONDITIONS AND VISIBILITY AT TIME OF CRASH OR WHEN LAST REPORTED:
      Unknown
   4. GIVE: (a) Day 12  Month Mar  Year 1945  Time 1045  and Location Elmore Strip
      of last known whereabouts of missing aircraft.
      (b) Specify whether aircraft was last sighted (X); Last contacted by
      radio ( ); Forced down ( ); Seen to Crash ( ); or Information not Available ( );
   5. AIRCRAFT WAS LOST, OR IS BELIEVED TO HAVE BEEN LOST, AS A RESULT OF: (Check
      only one)  Enemy Aircraft ( ); Enemy Anti-Aircraft ( ); Other Circumstances as
      follows:  Weather
   6. AIRCRAFT: Type, Model and Series  C-46D    ; AAF Serial Number  44-77373
   7. NICKNAME OF AIRCRAFT, If any    None
   8. ENGINES: Type, Model and Series  P & W R2800-51  ; AAF Serial Number
      (a) Left         (b) FP-081985     ; (c)           ; (d)
   9. INSTALLED WEAPONS (Furnish below Make, Type and Serial Number):
      (a)  2 Thompson Sub-Machine Guns  ; (b)           ; (c)
  10. THE PERSONS LISTED BELOW WERE REPORTED AS:  (a) Battle Casualty
                            or (b) Non Battle Casualty     X
  11. NUMBER OF PERSONS ABOARD AIRCRAFT: Crew  4  Passengers Unknown ; Total Unknown
      (Starting with Pilot, furnish the following particulars: If more than 11 persons
      were aboard aircraft, list similar particulars on separate sheet and attach ori-
      ginal to this form.)
                        Name in Full                Serial     Current
         Crew Position  (Last Name First)   Grade   Number     Status
DED 1.   Pilot          Kelly, Leo J.       2nd Lt. 0-899426   Missing
DED 2.   Co-pilot       Healy, Paul A.      2nd Lt. 0-769437   Missing
DED 3.   Engineer       Oja, Theodore R.    Sgt.    17158005   Missing
DEP 4.   Radio Operator Klester, Charles W. S/Sgt.  33080528   Missing
     5.  See attachment for list of medical attendants and patients.
     6.
     7.
     8.
     9.
    10.
    11.
```

Missing Air Crew Report 13672, Mindoro, dated 12 Mar 1945. *National Archives and Records Administration,*

~~CONFIDENTIAL~~

12. IDENTIFY BELOW THOSE PERSONS WHO ARE BELIEVED TO HAVE LAST KNOWLEDGE OF AIRCRAFT, AND CHECK APPROPRIATE COLUMN TO INDICATE BASIS FOR SAME:

Check only one Column

Name in Full (Last Name First)	Grade	Serial Number	Contacted by Radio	Last Sighted	Saw Crash	Forced Landing
1. Daugherty, Robert W.	2nd Lt.	O-820962		X		
2. Operations Officer, Elmore Strip.			X			

13. IF PERSONNEL ARE BELIEVED TO HAVE SURVIVED, ANSWER YES TO ONE OF THE FOLLOWING STATEMENTS: (a) Parachutes were used ____; (b) Persons were seen walking away from scene of crash ____; or (c) Any other reason (Specify) Unknown

14. ATTACH AERIAL PHOTOGRAPH, MAP, CHART OR SKETCH, SHOWING APPROXIMATE LOCATION WHERE AIRCRAFT WAS LAST SEEN OR HEARD FROM (Airplane was last seen at Elmore Strip, Mindoro, therefore map, chart, etc. not pertinent.

15. ATTACH EYEWITNESS DESCRIPTION OF CRASH, FORCED LANDING, OR OTHER CIRCUMSTANCES PERTAINING TO MISSING AIRCRAFT. (See Attachment No. 1)

16. GIVE NAME, GRADE AND SERIAL NUMBER OF OFFICER IN CHARGE OF **SEARCH**, IF ANY, INCLUDING DESCRIPTION AND EXTENT No search has been made yet due to weather, but queries have been sent out through AACS, 433rd Troop Carrier Group, and 54th Troop Carrier Wing.

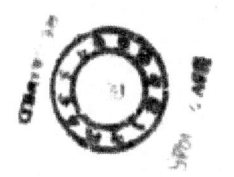

Date of Report 13 March, 1945.

(Signature of Presenting Officer)
RALPH C. ALEXANDER,
Captain, Air Corps,
Commanding.

17. REMARKS OR EYEWITNESS STATEMENTS: (See attachments)

3 ATTACHMENTS:
1. Statement of 2nd Lt. Robert W. Daugherty.
2. Statement of 1st Lt. Bruce L. Marble
3. Message from 69th Sq. to Elmore Strip.
4. List of patients and medical personnel aboard A/c.

Incl. 1

-2-

Missing Air Crew Report 13672, Mindoro, dated 12 Mar 1945. National Archives and Records Administration,

58 Organizational Records

HEADQUARTERS
54TH TROOP CARRIER WING
APO 248

MEDICAL PERSONNEL ABOARD X366, MISSING 12 MARCH 1945

STATUS	NAME	RANK	ASN	ORGN
	Medical Attendants:			
	Manler, Beatrice N.	2nd Lt.	N-788562	804th NAES
	Hudson, John H.	T/3	18216869	804th NAES
	Patients			
DNB	1. Adamsky, Thomas (NMI)	Pfc	33395514	Hqs 21st Inf Regt
DNB	2. Gots, Fabian T.	T/4	39842703	Hq & Sv 658 Amph Trac Bn
DNB	3. Ingalls, Phillip	Pvt	32472946	13th Sta Hosp
DNB	4. Sintic, Joseph E.	Pvt	35919729	21st Inf Regt
DNB	5. Jahnke, Ray S.	Pfc	36025969	D 186th Inf Regt
DNB	6. Meagher, Harry B.	Pvt	39328703	405 Sig Co Avn
DNB	7. Srel, Gerald P.	Pvt	31383697	3144 Sig Sv Det
DNB	8. Mills, Charles L.	T/4	37158737	1458 AIN
DNB	9. Kvist, Alfred J.	Pfc	36265182	Hqs 34th Inf Regt
DNB	10. Wells, George E.	Sgt	18097552	C 511 Para Inf
DNB	11. Najecki, Edward J.	Pfc	32357358	A 3 Engr Bn (C)
	12. Clarke, Matthew J.	Sgt	20229802	C 19th Inf
DNB	13. Hankerson, John E.	Sgt	34719572	1938 Ordn Co
DNB	14. Howard, Ralph H.	Cpl	14185538	35 Ftr Sq 5 Ftr Gp
DNB	15. Wynn, James L.	T/5	16630578	E 543 EB & SR
DNB	16. Anger, William F.	T/5	39142267	B 658 Amph Trac Bn
**	17. Magboo, Maximo	Pvt		Co B 5th Phil-Amer Army
DNB	18. Johnes, Hurtle	Pfc	34730913	K 162 Inf Regt
DNB	19. Turner, Lytle I.	Pfc	35917725	PCAU 23 USAFFE
*	20. Avers, William N.	Cpl	835152	MAG 32 USMC
DNB	21. Weltick, Harold W.	Pfc	32689091	C 186 Inf Regt
DNB	22. Bishop, Audie H.	Sgt	13036741	303 A D Sq
*	23. Zakrzewski, Rudolph L.	S 1/c	700-92-65	USCG LST #18
DNB	24. Twitchell, James R.	Pfc	39525522	41st Sig Corps
DNB	25. Gilley, Paul E.	Pfc	13117368	543 EB & SR
DNB	26. Collins, Clyde C.	T/5	36264632	Btry B 102 AAA
DNB	27. Fredrickson, Virgil H.	Pvt	37518702	Btry A 102 AAA
DNB	28. White, Clarence H.	Pvt	36218926	5237 Sig Co

* Not U.S. Army personnel
** Not U.S. Personnel

Missing Air Crew Report 13672, Mindoro, dated 12 Mar 1945. National Archives and Records Administration,

CONFIDENTIAL
ATTACHMENT NO. 1 TO MISSING AIR CREW REPORT

HEADQUARTERS
69TH TROOP CARRIER SQUADRON
433RD TROOP CARRIER GROUP, AAF
APO 72

13 March, 1945.

Statement of 2nd Lt. Robert W. Daugherty on XA366.

On 12 March, 1945 about 1045, I observed XA366 with Lt. Kelly and Lt. Healy taking off at Elmore Strip for Tanauan. Previous to his take-off I had talked to them and found out they were taking Air Evacs to Leyte.

At approximately 1300 to 1330, while enroute to Leyte, my radio operator, Sgt. Ray W. Williams, 34435399, reported that he had heard XA366 say he was turning back to Mindoro. That was the last contact we heard from them.

ROBERT W. DAUGHERTY,
2nd Lt. Air Corps,
Pilot.

Attachment 1

CONFIDENTIAL

Missing Air Crew Report 13672, Mindoro, dated 12 Mar 1945. National Archives and Records Administration,

60 Organizational Records

From	8 JANUARY 1945 Date and Hour		JOHN M. OP 357th INFANTRY	OSPERN P6834 Location of Headquarters BA VIGNE P6449
To	8 JANUARY 1945 Date and Hour			
Time In	Time Out	Serial No.	Time Dated	Incidents, messages, orders, etc.	Action taken
			1200	Rear units moved north out of OSPERN preparatory to assuming positions for attack scheduled for 9th.	
			1900	The following positions have been taken by the regiment: 1st Bn, vicinity WINZERWEG; 2nd Bn, BAVIGNE; 3rd Bn, LEIFRANGE. Regtl Cp and special units at BAVIGNE, all units in these positions by 1850. Division FO #48, summarized, calls for following action: III Corps attacks at 091000A to eliminate enemy pocket southeast of BASTOGNE. 90th Div attacks through elements of 26th Division, to seize high ground vicinity of BRAS, maintaining contact with the 26th Div on the right and TF SCOTT on the left. Regimental Field Order #23, summarized: Attachments: Co A 773rd TD Bn; Co C 712th Tk Bn; Co C, 3rd Cml Bn; 90th Rcn Troop; Co A (-) 315th Engrs; Co A 315 Med Bn. Attacks two battalions abreast, 1st on right, attacking with A Company; 2nd Bn on left attacking with E and F Cos. 1st Bn to seize initial objective on right, including town of BERLE, ready to continue on order. 2nd Bn, seize initial objective on left and be prepared to advance on order. 3rd Bn to move forward from present area to WILTZERWEG beginning at 0930, being prepared to pass through either of the assault battalions and continue the attk. 90th Rcn to maintain contact between our second battalion and TF SCOTT on the left. The two assaulting battalions have one platoon each of the following: TDs, Tks, Cml Morters, Engrs. 3rd Bn has same except for Engrs. Objectives set up in the division overlay were, roughly: Initial, including the towns of BERLE and TRENTHOF (in 359 area). Intermediate objective, the high ground immediately south of the town of DONCOLS and SONLEZ; final, oval including the towns DONCOLS and BRAS.	
			2400	Nothing further at this hour.	

90th Division, 357th Infantry Unit Journal January 1945. National Personnel Records Center, College Park, MD.

5

Military Death Records

62 *Military Death Records*

Military service records are not the only records through which we can learn about the life of a soldier. Sadly many soldiers did not make it back alive and a separate record set exists for them.

If your soldier was identified, one of the first records you should request is the Individual Deceased Personnel Files (IDPF.) Identified means two things where an IDPF is concerned. First, he or she was buried overseas in an American Battle Monuments Commission Cemetery or was buried stateside, and you can locate the soldier's name on a list. Second, if your soldier was listed as Missing in Action (MIA) and later officially declared deceased and deemed unrecoverable, there will be an IDPF.

The Office of the Quartermaster Graves Registration Service (GRS) created IDPFs for soldiers who died state-side and overseas. These records do not exist for soldiers who died after their military service ended.

Now, if your soldier was listed as MIA then declared deceased and possibly recovered but unidentified, there will be an X-File. What is the difference between an IDPF and an X-File and why does it matter if a soldier was identified? Let's take a closer look at these files to figure that out.

The IDPF for an identified soldier contains the name, rank, and serial number of the soldier. Soldiers who did not have any personal effects or identification tags or other items to help identify them had no serial number. When they were recovered and buried in the military cemeteries, they were given an X-number to replace their serial number. The X-number was the next number of burial in that particular cemetery.

In cases where remains were disinterred and enough information was brought forth to aid in identification, the X-File would be combined into a full IDPF. Both files contain similar records but the main difference is whether or not the soldier was identifiable.

IDPFs can be ordered through Fort Knox and details are found within this chapter. X-Files are of course not indexed by a soldier's name and it is nearly impossible to find a potential match without a great deal of research. More will be discussed on these files in my book *Volume II: Navigating World War II Accident Reports, Internment and Prisoner Records, and Death Records* due for release mid-2015.

Individual Deceased Personnel File (IDPF) and X-File Contents

An Individual Deceased Personnel File (IDPF) was created for every soldier received by the Graves Registration Service (GRS.)

Each document within an IDPF contains the name, rank, serial number, and unit. The X-File forms contained the X-number on every form. Both file types range from approximately 15-20 pages to over 150 depending on the contents. The primary documents are explored within this guide. A more detailed description can be found in my next book Stories from the Battlefield.

A **Report of Burial** contained the soldier's name, service number, rank, and date and place of death. An addressograph machine was used to stamp a copy of his identification tag onto this form. The grave location with the name, serial number, rank, unit, and grave number of the individuals to the right and left of the soldier are included.

Any personal effects collected off the remains at the time of receipt were noted on this form and sent to the Quartermaster Depot in Kansas City for processing and shipment to the next of kin. Often personal effects were stored in a duffle bag or other bag with the unit elsewhere to be retrieved later for processing. It is possible a family received multiple shipments of personal effects due to the timing of processing both on the battlefield and in Kansas City.

If Deceased was Unidentified

If the deceased was unidentified, a file similar to the IDPF was created. This is called the X-File. It contains a Report of Burial, search and recovery information, and dental examination records. The GRS then contacted the War Department for physical and dental examination records from a soldier's personnel file for comparison against the remains if enough evidence existed to possibly identify a soldier.

How could a soldier be identified by the GRS if no identification tags or personal effects were with the remains? Research was conducted into the units who fought in the area where the remains were recovered. Morning Reports would be consulted to determine which soldiers were killed in that area. Those not recovered would have files pulled to compare current information on physical and dental characteristics to personnel files.

The **Battle Casualty Report** designated a soldier as Missing in Action (MIA) or Killed in Action (KIA.) These reports also contain the name of the next of kin and relationship to the deceased as well as the date notified of the casualty.

The **Report of Death** was a form for the Adjutant General's Office which listed the deceased's usual information, branch of service, date of birth and death, date of active entry in service, where he was killed, emergency contact and beneficiary information. This form was sent to the War Department. Then a telegram and official letter was sent to the family of the deceased.

The **Inventory of Effects** form described the personal effects collected by the GRS to be sent to the family. These effects were first sent to the Quartermaster Effects Depot in Kansas City, Missouri for processing. After processing, the effects and a letter were sent to the next of kin. In some cases, the next of kin would respond by handwritten letter acknowledging receipt of these items and asking about additional items not received.

The **Request for Disposition of Remains** was sent to the next of kin to complete and return to the War Department. The next of kin had to indicate how they wished the remains to be permanently interred. The choices were:

- To be interred at a Permanent American Military Cemetery Overseas.

- To be returned to the United States or any possession or territory thereof for interment by next of kin in a private cemetery.

- To be returned to [insert foreign country] the homeland of the deceased for interment by next of kin.

- To be returned to the United States for final interment in a National Cemetery.

The **Disinterment Directive** form contained the basic identifying information on the Soldier Dead: Name, rank, service number, date of death, cemetery name and location of grave, name and address of next of kin, condition of remains, date disinterred and remains prepared.

Requesting IDPFs

IDPFs are free and take at least six months to receive. Mark your calendar when you mail the letter requesting the file. To request an IDPF you can use the sample letter provided below and complete as much information as possible.

The Army Air Corps IDPFs are now held at the NPRC in St. Louis, although it is hit or miss. You can try sending a letter to the NPRC but I also suggest you send the same letter to Fort Knox.

National Personnel Records Center
1 Archives Drive
St. Louis, Missouri 63138

For all other branches, write to the following address:

U.S. Army Human Resources Command
ATTN: AHRC-PAO (Dept. 103)
1600 Spearhead Division Avenue
Fort Knox, KY 40122

Example IDPF Request Letter

Dear Staff:

Pursuant to the Freedom of Information Act, I hereby make a request for the IDPF for my below listed family member who died or was killed-in-action while serving in the military during World War II.

Soldier's Name:
Branch of Military:
Military Service Number:
Division:
Date of Birth:
Date of Death:
Burial site in U.S.A.:
Buried:
Relationship to deceased:

Very truly yours,
Jane/Joe Genealogy

Military Headstone Application

The Military Headstone Application form was completed by the family after the Soldier Dead was repatriated. After the burial had taken place, the family was sent a headstone application that already contained the soldier's service number, name, and branch of the service. Stamped on the form was the cemetery name and city of nearest freight station for delivery.

The family had to complete the following fields on that form:

- Type of Marker

- Enlistment Date and Discharge Date (the discharge date was the death date)

- State of residence

- Regiment and company

- Birth and death dates

- Signature of family member with the date of application and address

Researchers are always told to check all the facts. Never believe everything you hear or see, even when it is written in stone. Case in point is Frank Winkler who served in World War II in the 29th Infantry Division, 115th Infantry Regiment, Co G. Yet his military issued headstone does not state this information. It states he served in the 129th Infantry, not the 29th.

Where did the mix-up occur? It was listed on the Military Headstone Application as 129th Infantry, completed by his father. The Army did not check the information provided by the family before issuing the headstone. They just issued based on what was on the application. How did I discover that what was on his grave was not the actual unit? The IDPF contained the correct information as did information provided by the Historian for the 29th Infantry Division. It is always helpful to contact the division historian if one exists to gather additional information. The headstone applications are available through Ancestry.com (subscription site) in digital format.

REPORT OF BURIAL

TM 10-630 AND AR 30-1815

Date: 17 Jan 45

PROVOZNIK	James	F	Pfc		36640529
Last Name	First	Initial	Rank		Serial No.

358th Inf — Unit
90th Div — Organization

Bras Belgium	UNK (Estimated 15 Jan 45)	HE Shell – Lower Trunk & Thigh Mangled
Place of Death	Date of Death	Cause of Death

1100 17 Jan 45 — Time and Date of Burial
U S Military Cemetery Hamm Luxembourg — Name of Cemetery / Location

265	11	L	Cross
Grave Number	Row Number	Plot Number	Type of Marker

Disposition of Identification Tags: Buried with body Yes ☒ No ☐ Attached to Marker Yes ☒ No ☐

If No Identification Tags – How were remains identified?

What means of identification were buried with the body?

To determine Right or Left use **Deceased's Right and Left.**

Who is buried on:

Deceased's Right: SAKSVIG 36006616 Cpl 358th Inf 90th Div 264

Deceased's Left: CHANDLER 38282774 Pvt 358th Inf 90th Div 266

Signature or Name, Rank and if possible Organization of person furnishing above Data when other than officer reporting burial.

JAMES F PRIVOZNIK
36640529 T43-43 O
C

If print of identification tag is not affixed fill in below:

Emergency Addressee: UNKNOWN

Address:

Religion: Catholic

List only Personal Effects **Found on Body** and disposition of same:

No personal effects.

#243 Provoznik, James J. 36,640,529

For The Commanding Officer
CARL D TRUAX
1st Lt QMC   Verified by G.R.S. Officer
609th QM Gr Reg Co

RESTRICTED

United States Army, Individual Deceased Personnel File, U.S. Army Human Resources Command, Fort Knox, KY, Report of Burial for James F Privoznik, serial no. 36640529, dated 17 Jan 1945, stamped Commanding Office of Graves Registration Company Mar 1945.

Military Death Records

WAR DEPARTMENT
THE ADJUTANT GENERAL'S OFFICE
WASHINGTON 25, D. C.

—BATTLE CASUALTY REPORT— 144512

NAME	SERIAL NUMBER	GRADE	ARM OR SERVICE	REPORTING THEATRE
WINKLER FRANK J	36695605	PVT	INF	ETO

PLACE OF CASUALTY	DATE OF CASUALTY (DAY/MONTH/YEAR)	FLYING OR JUMPING STAT	TYPE OF CASUALTY	SHIPMENT NUMBER
FRANCE	24 JUN 44		MIA	133

NAME AND ADDRESS OF EMERGENCY ADDRESSEE

THE INDIVIDUAL NAMED ABOVE DESIGNATED THE FOLLOWING PERSON AS THE ONE TO BE NOTIFIED IN CASE OF EMERGENCY, AND THE OFFICIAL TELEGRAPHIC AND LETTER NOTIFICATIONS WILL BE SENT TO THIS PERSON. THE RELATIONSHIP, IF ANY, IS SHOWN BELOW. IT SHOULD BE NOTED THAT THIS PERSON IS NOT NECESSARILY THE NEXT-OF-KIN OR RELATIVE DESIGNATED TO BE PAID SIX MONTHS' PAY GRATUITY IN CASE OF DEATH

MR.-MRS.-MISS—FIRST NAME—MIDDLE INITIAL—LAST NAME	RELATIONSHIP	DATE NOTIFIED
MRS. JENNIE K WINKLER	MOTHER	25 July 1944

NO. AND NAME OF STREET—CITY—STATE
4134 WEST 31st STREET CHICAGO ILLINOIS

REMARKS: CORRECTED COPY oli

United States Army, Individual Deceased Personnel File, U.S. Army Human Resources Command, Fort Knox, KY, Battle Casualty Report for Frank Winkler serial no. 36695605, dated 24 July 1944.

WAR DEPARTMENT
THE ADJUTANT GENERAL'S OFFICE
WASHINGTON 25, D. C.

396327

REPORT OF DEATH   DATE 3 February 1945

FULL NAME Privoznik, James F.	**ARMY SERIAL NUMBER** 36 640 529	**GRADE** DCS/4632 PFC
HOME ADDRESS Chicago, Illinois	**ARM OR SERVICE** Infantry	**DATE OF BIRTH** 30 July 21
PLACE OF DEATH European area	**CAUSE OF DEATH** Killed in action	**DATE OF DEATH** 11 Jan 45
STATION OF DECEASED European area	**DATE OF ENTRY ON CURRENT ACTIVE SERVICE** 10 Feb 43	**LENGTH OF SERVICE FOR PAY PURPOSES** YEARS MONTHS DAYS

EMERGENCY ADDRESSEE (NAME, RELATIONSHIP & ADDRESS)
Mrs. Mary Privoznik, mother, 3124 South Ridgeway Ave., Chicago, Illinois

BENEFICIARY (NAME, RELATIONSHIP & ADDRESS)
Mary Privoznik, mother, same as above
Leroy Privoznik, brother, same as mother's

INVESTIGATION MADE?	IN LINE OF DUTY	OWN MISCONDUCT	WAS DECEASED ON DUTY STATUS	AUTHORIZED ABSENCE	IN FLYING PAY STATUS	OTHER PAY STATUS (SPECIFY BELOW)
YES NO	YES NO	YES NO	YES NO	YES NO	YES NO	YES NO X

ADDITIONAL DATA AND/OR STATEMENT
Evidence of death rec'd in WD 27 Jan 45   [X] BATTLE   [ ] NON-BATTLE

BY ORDER OF THE SECRETARY OF WAR

United States Army, Individual Deceased Personnel File, U.S. Army Human Resources Command, Fort Knox, KY, Report of Death for James F Privoznik, serial no. 36640529, dated 3 Feb 1945.

Military Death Records

Sheet ___ of ___ Sheets	ARMY EFFECTS BUREAU	Deceased ✓
Box No. ___		Missing ___
	INVENTORY Box 64	P.O.W. ___
		Abandoned ___

SHOWN ON TALLY-IN AS: *Fred A. Davis*   ORIGINAL NO. OF PKGS. ___

TALLY-IN NO. 5152   INVENTORY DATE 10/14/44   CASE NO. 39668 US

EFFECTS OF: *Fred A. Davis*   RANK Lt.

A.S.N. O-683416   ORG. Unknown

PACKAGE DESCRIPTION: #1 carton

ARTICLE DESCRIPTION

- 1 Barrack Bag
- 1 Towel
- 1 Tie
- 1 shirt
- 1 pr swim trunks
- 1 pr tennis shoes
- 1 pr socks
- 1 sweat suit

REMARKS: Rechecked
no information
C.A.I. not available
no correspondence
Shortage on reverse

ATTACHMENTS: 2 inventory

NO CORRESPONDENCE
SHORTAGE ON REVERSE
G.I. ON REVERSE

STORAGE SPACE: 548

SAFE STORAGE / VAULT STORAGE

WEIGHT SHIPPED: NOV 1

United States Army, Individual Deceased Personnel File, U.S. Army Human Resources Command, Fort Knox, KY, Inventory of Personal Effects for Fred Davis serial no. O-683416, dated 14 Oct 1944.

2/Lt Fred A. Davis, O 683 416
Plot MMM, Row 3, Grave 68,
United States Military Cemetery
St. Avold, France

9 December 1948

Mrs. Elsie J. Sherrill
532 West 60th Street
Chicago, Illinois

Dear Mrs. Sherrill:

    The people of the United States, through the Congress have authorized the disinterment and final burial of the heroic dead of World War II. The Quartermaster General of the Army has been entrusted with this sacred responsibility to the honored dead. The records of the War Department indicate that you may be the nearest relative of the above-named deceased, who gave his life in the service of his country.

    The enclosed pamphlets, "Disposition of World War II Armed Forces Dead," and "American Cemeteries," explain the disposition, options and services made available to you by your Government. If you are the next of kin according to the line of kinship as set forth in the enclosed pamphlet, "Disposition of World War II Armed Forces Dead," you are invited to express your wishes as to the disposition of the remains of the deceased by completing Part I of the enclosed form "Request for Disposition of Remains." Should you desire to relinquish your rights to the next in line of kinship, please complete Part II of the enclosed form. If you are not the next of kin, please complete Part III of the enclosed form.

    If you should elect Option 2, it is advised that no funeral arrangements or other personal arrangements be made until you are further notified by this office.

    Will you please complete the enclosed form, "Request for Disposition of Remains" and mail in the enclosed self-addressed envelope, which requires no postage, within 30 days after its receipt by you? Its prompt return will avoid unnecessary delays.

Sincerely,

THOMAS B. LARKIN
Major General
The Quartermaster General

LOI Sent 9 DEC 1948

United States Army, Individual Deceased Personnel File, U.S. Army Human Resources Command, Fort Knox, KY, Disinterment Request Letter for Fred Davis serial no. O-683416, dated 9 Dec 1949.

72 Military Death Records

United States Army, Individual Deceased Personnel File, U.S. Army Human Resources Command, Fort Knox, KY, Disinterment Directive for Fred Davis serial no. O-683416, dated 15 Mar 1949.

Military Death Records

DISINTERMENT DIRECTIVE

SECTION A — NAME AND BURIAL LOCATION OF DECEASED

NAME	SERIAL NUMBER	RANK	ARM	DATE OF DEATH
DAVIS FRED A.	0-683416 ~~UNKNOWN X-007704~~	2 LT		

CEMETERY:

DISPOSITION OF REMAINS:

PLOT	ROW	GRAVE	COUNTRY	CAUSE OF DEATH
4 M	3	68	ST AVOLD FRANCE	

SECTION B — CONSIGNEE AND NEXT OF KIN

NAME AND ADDRESS OF CONSIGNEE:

NAME AND ADDRESS OF NEXT OF KIN:

SECTION C — DISINTERMENT AND IDENTIFICATION

NAME	SERIAL NUMBER	RANK	DATE OF DEATH	DATE DISINTERRED
DAVIS, Fred A	0-683416	2 Lt	2 Nov 47	30 Mar 48

IDENTIFICATION TAG ON: [ ] REMAINS [X] MARKER EMB
ORGANIZATION:
RELIGION: Unk
IDENTIFICATION VERIFIED BY: Oliver E Modin, Embalmer

SECTION D — PREPARATION OF REMAINS FOR SHIPMENT

NATURE OF BURIAL: Uniform
CONDITION OF REMAINS: Crushed skull. Multiple fractures.

OTHER MEANS OF IDENTIFICATION: Report of Burial found on remains, reads: "UNK X -7704".

MINOR DISCREPANCIES: None

REMAINS PREPARED AND PLACED IN CASKET

DATE: 2 Apr 48
CASKET SEALED BY: Oliver E Modin, Embalmer
EMBALMER (Signature): Oliver E Modin, Embalmer
CASKET BOXED AND MARKED
DATE: 2 Apr 48 BY Oliver E Modin, Embalmer
All markings, tags and plates verified by Bruce E Blair, 1st Lt QMC

I hereby certify that all the foregoing operations were conducted and accomplished under my immediate supervision and that the report above is correct.

Bruce E Blair, 1st Lt QMC, 337 QM Bn
SIGNATURE OF GRS INSPECTOR

Prepare Discrepancy Report QMC Form 1194a for major discrepancies.

QMC FORM REV 15 MAR 46 1194

United States Army, Individual Deceased Personnel File, U.S. Army Human Resources Command, Fort Knox, KY, Disinterment Directive for Fred Davis serial no. O-683416, dated 15 Mar 1949.

6

After The War

76 After the War

When the war ended and soldiers returned home, they were encouraged to file their Discharge papers with their County Recorder or County Clerk for safekeeping. This is one place to check for these records if you do not have them in your possession.

Some soldiers took advantage of the G.I. Bill and went to college. Look for records at colleges and universities, yearbooks, and within their special collections for materials.

Veterans' organizations and group sprung up after the war and many of these groups continue meeting annually today even though the veterans are fewer in number. Often these organizations have websites with digitized copies of records, books written by veterans, and other research materials.

Look for newspapers and obituaries over time. Often these will list service information.

Finally, if the veteran in your family is still alive, consider an oral history interview to capture the story of their life, their service and any other details they wish future generations to know. Alternatively, if you research and write the story of your soldier who has passed away or was killed in action, listening to oral histories of soldiers within the same unit or battle can provide great contextual detail.

For More Information and Advanced Research

The purpose of this guide was to give you a quick instruction on World War II records and resources. There are many topics which were not covered in this guide that will be discussed in the upcoming series Stories from the Battlefield, a multi-volume set of books exploring all military branches and the records for World War II.

Volume I: Navigating World War II Home Front, Civilian, Army, and Air Corps Records
Release date Spring 2015

Volume II: Navigating World War II Accident Reports, Internment and Prisoner Records, and Death Records
Anticipated release late Summer 2015

Volume III: Navigating World War II Navy, Coast Guard, Marine Corps, and Merchant Marine Records
Anticipated release Fall 2015

Volume IV: Navigating World War II National Guard Records
Anticipated release Fall 2015

In these volumes I will cover the topics of historical context as it relates to the war, home front life, women in the military, Prisoner of War records (in the U.S. and overseas,) Internment Records (in the U.S. and overseas), African Americans in the War, Jews and the Holocaust, and provide an in-depth examination of records and resources relating to each branch of the military. All of these resources and more will help you not only research your military ancestor's story but also write his story.

Do you still want more information on WWII records and resources? Subscribe to my newsletter, follow my Generations Blog, (http://blog.generationsbiz.com) or attend one of my military lectures in the Chicago area.

Have questions or need some assistance with research and writing or want to book a WWII lecture? Please email me for services and fees. jenniferholik@generationsbiz.com

Selected Resources

World War II Toolbox

Visit my website for an extensive listing of World War II websites and online books.

http://jenniferholik.com

Books

Gawne, Jonathan. *Finding Your Father's War.* Philadelphia: Casemate, 2013.

Knox, Debra Johnson. *World War II Military Records.* Spartanburg: Military Information Enterprises, Inc., 2003.

Neagles, James . *U.S. Military Records: A Guide to Federal & State Sources.* Provo: Ancestry Publishing, 1994.

Pfeiffer, Laura Szucs. *Hidden Sources Family* History in Unlikely Places. Orem: Ancestry Publishing, 2000.

Sledge, Michael. *Soldier Dead. How We Recover, Identify, Bury, and Honor Our Military Fallen.* New York: Columbia University Press, 2005.

Steere, Edward. *The Graves Registration Service in World War II.* Washington D.C.: U.S. Government Printing Office, 1951.

Steere, Edward and Boardman, Thayer M. *Final Disposition of World War II Dead 1945-1951.* Washington D.C.: Historical Branch of the Office of the Quartermaster General, 1957.

Szucs, Loretto Dennis, and Luebking, Sandra Hargreaves, eds. *The Source A Guidebook to American Genealogy.* Provo: The Generations Network, 2006.

Weatherford, Doris. *American Women and World War II.* New York: Facts on File, 1990.

Yellin, Emily. *Our Mothers' War.* New York: Free Press, 2004.

Index

Index

After Action Reports 11, 20, 24, 48, 49
Air Force Accident Reports 11, 20, 48, 50
American Battle Monuments Commission 24, 25, 62

Cemetery 11, 20, 25, 26, 62, 64
Correspondence 11, 20, 33, 48, 53

Discharge Papers 20, 21, 24, 25, 31, 66, 76

Field Manuals 48, 54

General Orders 11, 20, 48, 52
Graves Registration Service 62, 63, 80

Home Sources 11, 20, 26

IDPF 11, 20, 21, 25, 30, 31, 49, 52, 54, 62, 63, 65, 66
Individual Deceased Personnel File 11, 20, 21, 25, 54, 63, 67, 68, 69, 70, 71, 72, 73
Individual Deceased Personnel File (IDPF) 67, 68, 69, 70, 71, 72, 73

Maps 11, 20, 24, 48, 51, 53
Military Headstone Application 11, 66
Missing Air Crew Reports 11, 20, 48, 51
Morning Reports 11, 20, 24, 32, 48, 49, 52, 63

National Personnel Records Center 9, 17, 24, 27, 32, 35, 36, 37, 38, 39, 40, 41, 42, 43, 44, 45, 55, 60, 65

Official Military Personnel File 11, 20, 29, 30, 35, 36, 37, 38, 39, 40, 41, 42, 43, 44, 45

Photographs 11, 20, 26, 48, 53

Red Cross 11, 30, 33, 34
Report of Burial 67, 68, 69, 70, 71, 72, 73

Separation Papers 20, 26
Service Number 11, 24, 65
Staff Reports 11, 20, 48, 52
Stars and Stripes 54

Technical Manuals 54
Training Manuals 48, 54

United Service Organization 11, 34
Unit Histories 11, 20, 24, 26, 31, 48, 52

YANK Magazine 54

About the Author

About The Author

Jennifer is a genealogical, historical, and military researcher. Through her business Generations, she lectures throughout the Chicagoland area on World War II records and stories, women during World War II, kids genealogy, and Italian genealogy.

As a researcher and writer she can help you research and piece together the stories of your ancestors, particularly if they served during World War II.

She is on the staff of the World War II History Network. You can join the community at http://wwiihistorynetwork.com

Jennifer volunteers as the Genealogy Department Manager at Casa Italia in Stone Park, Illinois. There she hosts monthly genealogy and writing programs and works in the Italian American Veterans Museum.

You can learn more about Jennifer and utilize her World War II Researcher's Toolbox at http://jenniferholik.com

Books By Author

All books and associated guides can be purchased through the author's website http://jenniferholik.com or on Amazon.

Military Books

The Tiger's Widow

Love knows no boundaries of time and space or life and death. It exists forever in our hearts as we remember and honor those who have gone before us. Through those memories we pass life lessons on to the next generation. We teach others there is light after darkness, hope after despair, and love is the glue that puts shattered hearts back together. This is a story of five hearts separated by time and space; hearts which would meet in the perfect moment. It is a story about never ending love that lived on even after death.

Join me on a journey that spans 72 years and several continents. This is the story of the life of Virginia Scharer Brouk, the wife of Flying Tiger, Robert Brouk. Virginia picked up the pieces of her life and joined the Women's Army Auxiliary Corps, later known as the Women's Army Corps (WAC,) to take up the fight after Robert was killed in a plane crash. Virginia's story is of life, loss, war, and the connection of hearts filled with love.

Stories of the Lost

Imagine sending your son off to war. Will he return unharmed, unchanged, and whole? How long will he be gone? Will the war last forever? Will he return? Standing in front of you at the railroad station is a young man in uniform. He looks so handsome, so strong, and full of life. You hug him tightly before he boards the train. You wave goodbye and he's gone.

Years later your son returns from the war. He arrives not walking off the train, but carried off in a flag draped casket. Dead almost four years now and buried in a foreign land, you did not know where he was buried for almost two years after he was killed. Your son is unable to tell his story of war. Who will tell his story?

This book is a collection of stories about my relatives who left by train to fight for our freedom and never returned. Three of the men were brought home after the war ended. One however, still sleeps in that foreign soil. It is also the recognition of the men who cared for them after death. The stories of the lost found through the military record.

To Soar with the Tigers

This is the story of Flying Tiger Robert Brouk, a Flight Leader in the 3rd Squadron of the American Volunteer Group. In the months prior to Pearl Harbor, until the disbandment of the American Volunteer Group in July 1942, the Flying Tigers valiantly fought the Japanese over the skies of Burma and China. This story contains Robert's complete war diary. The diary outlines his dramatic experiences from the moment he enlisted in the American Volunteer Group to its disbandment. His story also contains snapshots of the life he led upon his return to his home in Cicero, Illinois; a graphic account of his untimely death; and accounts of how Robert has been remembered through the years.

Genealogy Books

Branching Out: Genealogy for Students 1st-3rd Grade
Branching Out: Genealogy for Students 4th-8th Grade
Branching Out: Genealogy for High School Students
Branching Out: Genealogy for Adults

Are you looking for a how-to genealogy book that introduces the basics of research through easy to learn lessons? Then look no further. In Branching Out, a new series available from Generations, author and professional genealogist Jennifer Holik provides adults with the tools they need to learn how to research their family history. Through thirty fun and educational lessons, you will learn the foundations of genealogy and how to begin research. Each lesson contains a clearly defined goal, all necessary vocabulary, additional reading assignments, and lesson and homework assignments to extend understanding of the concept.

Engaging the Next Generation: A Guide for Genealogy Societies and Libraries

Engaging the Next Generation is written specifically for groups looking to create youth programs. This is a two-part book featuring one-hour and half-day youth program examples and the complete 4th-8th grade Branching Out set of thirty lessons. Part I allows genealogy societies and libraries to create youth programs based on example outlines, example speaking text, and project ideas in the book. Part II allows genealogy societies and libraries to build larger programs using the thirty lessons provided in the Branching Out series. Part II can also be used to teach beginning genealogy in public schools.